School Secretaries

by Mary Firestone

Consultant:
Kathleen A. Barclay
National Association of Educational Office Professionals
Former Editor of *The National Educational Secretary*

Bridgestone Books
an imprint of Capstone Press
Mankato, Minnesota

Bridgestone Books are published by Capstone Press.
151 Good Counsel Drive, P.O. Box 669, Mankato, Minnesota 56002
http://www.capstone-press.com

Copyright © 2003 by Capstone Press. All rights reserved.
No part of this publication may be reproduced in whole or in part, or stored in a retrieval system, or transmitted in any form or by any means, electronic, mechanical, photocopying, recording, or otherwise, without written permission of the publisher.
For information regarding permission, write to Capstone Press,
151 Good Counsel Drive, P.O. Box 669, Dept. R, Mankato, Minnesota 56002
Printed in the United States of America

Library of Congress Cataloging-in-Publication Data
Firestone, Mary.
   School secretaries/by Mary Firestone.
   v. cm—(Community helpers)
   Includes bibliographical references and index.
   Contents: School secretaries—What school secretaries do—Skills school secretaries need—Tools secretaries use—When school secretaries work—How secretaries learn—Where school secretaries work—People who help secretaries—How school secretaries help others—Hands on—Words to know.
   ISBN 0-7368-1617-8 (hardcover)
   1. School secretaries—Juvenile literature. [1. School secretaries. 2. Secretaries. 3. Occupations.] I. Title. II. Community helpers (Mankato, Minn.)
LB2844.4 .F57 2003
371.2—dc21   2002011105

Editorial Credits
Heather Adamson, editor; Karen Risch, product planning editor; Patrick D. Dentinger, cover production designer; Alta Schaffer, photo researcher

Photo Credits
All photos by Capstone Press/Jim Foell

1 2 3 4 5 6 08 07 06 05 04 03

Table of Contents

School Secretaries 5
What School Secretaries Do 7
Skills School Secretaries Need 9
Tools Secretaries Use 11
When School Secretaries Work 13
How Secretaries Learn 15
Where School Secretaries Work 17
People Who Help Secretaries 19
How School Secretaries Help Others 21
Hands On: Mixing Names 22
Words to Know 23
Read More 24
Internet Sites 24
Index 24

School Secretaries

Most schools have secretaries. School secretaries help students, teachers, and principals. They place student records in files and answer the phone. They make bus plans and welcome visitors.

What School Secretaries Do

School secretaries have many jobs. They type office letters. School secretaries keep track of the school budget. They arrange meetings for the principal and sort mail. Secretaries give messages and make announcements.

budget
a plan for spending money

Skills School Secretaries Need

School secretaries need many skills. They make sure important papers do not get lost. They need to speak and write well. Secretaries must know how to type and use a calculator.

Tools Secretaries Use

Secretaries have many tools to help them. They use computers and copy machines. They also use the Internet and e-mail. School secretaries sometimes use intercoms to give messages and make announcements.

intercom
a telephone and speaker system that allows you to talk and listen from room to room

When School Secretaries Work

Many school secretaries work eight hours a day. They begin an hour before the school day starts. Some secretaries are still working in the office after classes. Secretaries work at least part of the summer.

How Secretaries Learn

School secretaries learn their jobs in different ways. Some are trained in schools that teach office skills. Others go to workshops. Some secretaries learn by working on the job.

workshop
a meeting where people share ideas

Where School Secretaries Work

School secretaries usually work in school buildings. Their desks may be near the principal's office or near the school's entrance. Some secretaries work for several schools. They go to the schools when they are needed.

People Who Help Secretaries

Teachers' assistants and parents help secretaries. They make copies and put up displays. Translators tell secretaries what parents or students who speak a different language are saying.

translator
someone who puts words into another language

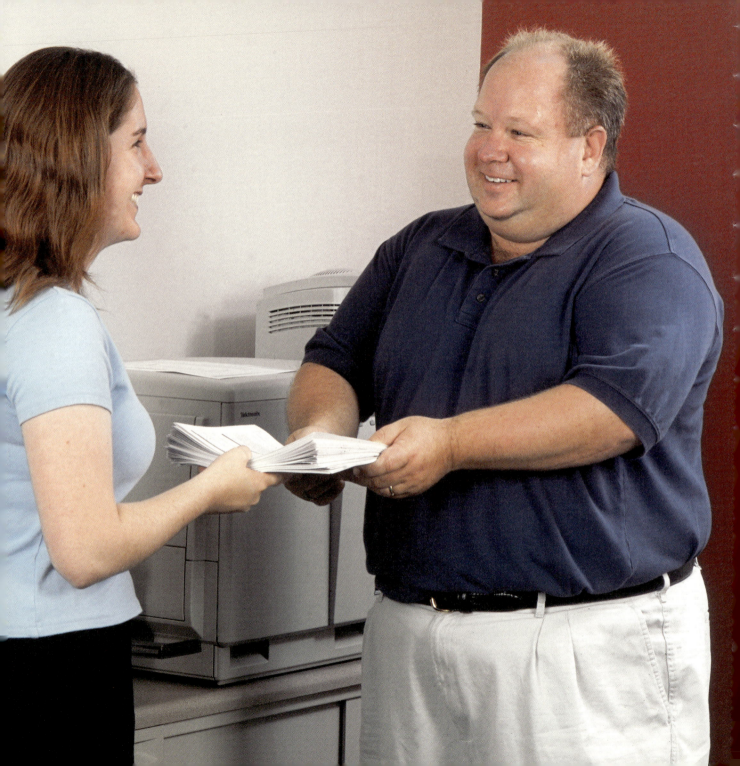

How School Secretaries Help Others

School secretaries help many people. Secretaries help teachers find things they need for class. They make visitors and students feel welcome. Secretaries help the school run smoothly.

Hands On: Mixing Names

Secretaries use the alphabet to stay organized. They keep student files in alphabetical order by using the first letter of the student's last name. If the first letters of two different names are the same, they go to the next letter in the name. You can practice alphabetizing like a secretary.

What You Need

a pencil
notecards
a paper bag
friends

What You Do

1. Think of six people. Write the last name of each person on a notecard. Write the first name of each person under his or her last name.
2. Place the notecards in the paper bag. Mix them up.
3. Have each person draw three cards. See who can put his or her cards in alphabetical order first. Try it again with more names.

Words to Know

assistant (uh-SISS-tuhnt)—someone who helps a leader with a project

budget (BUHJ-it)—a plan for spending money

calculator (KAL-kyuh-lay-tur)—a machine that does math problems quickly

intercom (IN-tur-kom)—a telephone and speaker system that allows you to talk and listen from room to room

translator (TRANSS-lay-tur)—someone who puts words into another language

workshop (WURK-shop)—a meeting where people share ideas

Read More

Boraas, Tracey. *School Principals.* Community Helpers. Mankato, Minn.: Bridgestone Books, 1999.

Klingel, Cindy, and Robert B. Noyed. *School Secretaries.* School Helpers. Vero Beach, Fla.: Rourke, 2001.

Internet Sites

Track down many sites about School Secretaries. Visit the FACT HOUND at *http://www.facthound.com*

IT IS EASY! IT IS FUN!

1) Go to *http://www.facthound.com*
2) Type in: 0736816178
3) Click on "FETCH IT" and FACT HOUND will find several links hand-picked by our editors.

Relax and let our pal FACT HOUND do the research for you!

Index

announcements, 7, 11
budget, 7
calculator, 9
computers, 11
letters, 7
meetings, 7
messages, 7, 11

principal, 5, 7, 17
school, 5, 13, 15, 17, 21
students, 5, 19, 21
summer, 13
teachers, 5, 21
type, 7, 9
visitors, 5, 21